Denbigh Castle

Denbigh Town Walls
Lord Leicester's Church
St Hilary's Chapel
Denbigh Friary

L. A. S. Butler MA, PhD, FSA

A History of Denbigh Castle

'The said castle is built upon a rock of stone, very stately and beautifully, in a very sweet air, seven miles from the sea; and near to the same castle are a few houses and a fair chapel'.

Extract from a survey made in the reign of King Henry VIII (1509–47).

Introduction

Denbigh Castle crowns the summit of a steep and prominent rock outcrop at the heart of the Vale of Clwyd. All too frequently overshadowed by the more famous strongholds of north-west Wales, Denbigh has a long and chequered history; its castellans were frequently caught up in events of regional and even national significance. It is a site, too, with several features of striking architectural ingenuity. The design of the great gatehouse in particular shows touches of considerable genius. Indeed, for the antiquary, John Leland (d. 1552), who examined the castle in the 1530s, had the gatehouse remained complete it 'might have counted among the most memorable peaces of workys yn England'.

Denbigh and North-East Wales Before King Edward I

The origins of Denbigh Castle lie in some 200 years of perennial warfare between Welsh princes and English kings during the eleventh and twelfth centuries. In particular, the princes of Gwynedd were determined to maintain a hold on the heart of their ancient kingdom — the region to the west of the river Conwy with its most secure of citadels, Snowdonia. In contrast, invading Norman barons, and later English kings, were attempting to contain any signs of independence on the part of the Welsh.

Between the river Conwy on the one hand and the Dee estuary on the other lay a large and vulnerable district. It was known variously as 'The Middle Country' (Y Berfeddwlad), because it lay between the two major Welsh kingdoms of Gwynedd and Powys, and as 'The Four Cantrefs', since it was composed of the four districts of Rhos, Rhufoniog (in which Denbigh lay), Dyffryn Clwyd and Tegeingl or Englefield. This was a border area, frequently fought over by the Welsh princes themselves.

It was also a natural target for English advance from Chester. Indeed, the pendulum of Welsh and English (or Norman) supremacy was to swing to and fro across this area for centuries. As early as the eighth century, King Offa (d. 796) raised the great dyke that bears his name, and separated his

Above: A coin of Offa, the powerful king of Mercia (d. 796). The great dyke that bears his name marked the border between his lands and those of the Welsh princes. The section shown here (below left) is close to Chirk Castle, near Wrexham (National Museum of Wales; Royal Commission on the Ancient and Historical Monuments of Wales).

Opposite: Denbigh Castle, begun in 1282, sits atop a steep rock outcrop at the heart of the Vale of Clwyd in that part of north Wales between the river Conwy and the Dee estuary that had been fought over for more than 200 years. The naturally strong location may have been the site of an early medieval fort, and under the Welsh princes there was certainly a royal residence, or llys, at Denbigh (RCAHMW).

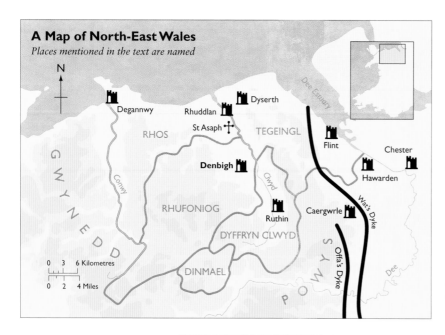

A Map of North-East Wales
Places mentioned in the text are named

Saxon kingdom of Mercia from the lands of the Welsh princes beyond. Regardless of its clear-cut nature, however, *Clawdd Offa* (as it was known to the Welsh) never really formed a permanent boundary. As the power of the princes waned, various settlers pushed westwards beyond the dyke and overran the coastal plain of north Wales, at least as far as the river Clwyd. In the tenth century it was the Saxons of Mercia, to be followed a century later by a renewed threat of land-hungry Normans advancing from Chester. So it was that Hugh of Avranches, first earl of Chester (d. 1101), and his kinsman, Robert 'of Rhuddlan' (d. 1088–93), pushed forward to the banks of the Clwyd and threw up a powerful castle mound near the mouth of the river at Rhuddlan.

Norman castles could not ensure permanent conquest and the Welsh princes — especially under the rulers of Gwynedd — gradually drove the invaders back in the twelfth century and occupied the

An imaginative reconstruction of the motte-and-bailey castle at Rhuddlan. Established in 1073, it was built near the mouth of the river Clwyd by Robert 'of Rhuddlan' (d. 1088–93), the lieutenant and kinsman of the Norman earl of Chester, Hugh of Avranches (d. 1101). During the lifetime of Earl Hugh, the Normans pushed along the north Wales coast deep into Gwynedd and planted similar fortresses at Caernarfon and at Aberlleiniog on Anglesey. These strongholds, however, could not prevent the resurgent Welsh princes from restoring their authority as far east as the Dee estuary during the twelfth century (Illustration by Terry Ball, 1989).

whole of north-east Wales to the Dee estuary. The pendulum of control continued to swing back and forth, and in 1247–56 the English once more gained the upper hand. During this period, Denbigh itself was under the control of King Henry III (1216–72), and further castles were built at Dyserth and Degannwy.

In short, if ever supremacy in north-east Wales was to rest firmly in English hands, it was necessary for additional castles to be built inland, probably in the broad fertile valleys, away from the immediate coastal plain. Indeed, in due course, castles were erected at Ruthin and at Denbigh.

The choice of Denbigh was not fortuitous. Its Welsh name, Dinbych, incorporates the word *dinas* (a rocky fortress), which suggests that it was long regarded as a natural stronghold; there may have been a fort here in the early medieval period. Under the Welsh princes, Denbigh was certainly a royal residence, a *llys*, supported by the services of bondmen — essentially a servile peasantry who provided labour in return for land. Indeed, in 1230, it was at Denbigh that the emissary of the chancellor of England visited the most powerful Welsh ruler, Llywelyn ab Iorwerth (Llywelyn the Great), prince of Gwynedd (d. 1240), to arrange a meeting at a mutually convenient place and time. They were to discuss the rival allegations of harassment made by Welsh and English tenants in the mid-Wales territories of Brecon and Builth — a measure of the extent of the Gwynedd prince's overlordship in much of Wales.

The English Conquest

In 1277 north-east Wales finally passed into English hands, when King Edward I (1272–1307) launched a determined offensive against the prince of Wales, Llywelyn ap Gruffudd (Llywelyn the Last, d. 1282), grandson of Llywelyn ab Iorwerth. The king's conquests went as far as the river Conwy, pushing the recalcitrant prince back into Snowdonia. Edward consolidated his own position by raising new castles at Rhuddlan and Flint. But under the terms of the political settlement, he also granted Llywelyn's brother, Dafydd ap Gruffudd (d. 1283), large areas between the Conwy and Clwyd rivers. Dafydd was to hold the two districts (or *cantrefi*) of Rhufoniog and Dyffryn Clwyd (thereby reviving an English grant

of 1263), and was even allowed to build the castle of Caergwrle (or Hope) with the knowledge and help of the king. This was a shrewd move by Edward I, because Dafydd — the youngest and most treacherous of Llywelyn's three brothers — had already twice defected to the English to secure their help against his brother. More recently, in November 1274, he had fled to the English court after the discovery of his plot to murder Llywelyn and rule Wales in his stead. The grant of Rhufoniog was to be Dafydd's opportunity to cause more trouble for his brother.

Above: This carved head, found at Degannwy Castle, near Conwy, may represent the powerful prince of Gwynedd, Llywelyn ab Iorwerth (Llywelyn the Great, d. 1240). He is known to have stayed at the royal llys *at Denbigh in 1230 (National Museum of Wales).*

Top left: The gilt-bronze tomb effigy of Henry III (1216–72) in Westminster Abbey. Capitalizing on the weakness of Gwynedd following Llywelyn ab Iorwerth's death, the king was able for a time to assert royal authority over The Four Cantrefs, including Denbigh (Courtesy of the Dean and Chapter of Westminster).

Left: The gains made by the English in the mid-thirteenth century were decisively reversed by Llywelyn ab Iorwerth's grandson, Llywelyn ap Gruffudd (Llywelyn the Last, d. 1282). Recognized as prince of Wales in 1267, the stability of his rule was repeatedly threatened by his treacherous younger brother, Dafydd (d. 1283). Their arms are depicted in the late thirteenth-century Lord Marshal's Roll *(Society of Antiquaries, London. Ms. 664, vol. iii, numbers 30 and 31).*

Above: King Edward I (1272–1307) in a marginal sketch from a contemporary manuscript. Edward twice went to war against Llywelyn ap Gruffudd — in 1276–77 and 1282–83. After the first war, which saw Llywelyn pushed back into Snowdonia, the heartland of Gwynedd, the king granted Dyffryn Clwyd and Rhufoniog, including Denbigh, to Llywelyn's troublesome brother, Dafydd (The National Archives: PRO, E 368/72).

King Edward I's Second Campaign in Wales 1282–83

N

Beaumaris
Rhuddlan
Flint
Conwy
Hawarden
Caernarfon
Denbigh
Chester
Northern Army
Criccieth
Ruthin
Dolwyddelan
Hope
Holt
Harlech
Chirk
Castell y Bere
Shrewsbury
Central Army
Montgomery
Aberystwyth

0   30 Kilometres
0   20 Miles

Builth

Southern Army
Carmarthen

Castles built or wholly rebuilt by King Edward I

Welsh castles repaired by King Edward I

Lordship castles built or rebuilt for King Edward I

Castles of the first war of Welsh independence, 1276–77

Castles of the second war of Welsh independence, 1282–83

Routes of Edward I's main armies in the second war of Welsh independence, 1282–83

Right: To consolidate the conquests made in north-east Wales during 1282, Edward I bestowed a number of new lordships upon trusted commanders. The lordship of Denbigh, made up of the cantrefi of Rhufoniog and Rhos, and the district of Dinmael, was granted to Henry de Lacy, earl of Lincoln (d. 1311). Lacy was one of the king's closest friends and a trusted royal servant. He had fought in both Welsh wars and his great seal shows him armed and mounted in a fashion befitting one of the great nobles of the late thirteenth century (British Library, Additional Charter 7438).

Denbigh stood in the *cantref* of Rhufoniog, and it was at this ancient princely seat that Dafydd established his principal stronghold. From a later survey, we know that he had a hall, private room, chapel, buttery and bakehouse within a court. It was from this powerbase that the discontented Dafydd swooped down upon the English stronghold at Hawarden Castle on Palm Sunday 1282, and threw the Welsh into open revolt against the English Crown. The underlying causes of disaffection were the tyrannical behaviour of English officials — especially Reginald Grey in north-east Wales — and the denial of Welsh laws and customs. But the immediate trigger may well have been the repair of Hawarden Castle by the English, in deliberate contravention of the terms of the 1267 Treaty of Montgomery, which had forbidden building work there for a period of thirty years. By launching this sudden attack, Dafydd forced his brother's hand: either support the rebellion or compromise his role as leader of the Welsh. Llywelyn ap Gruffudd joined his brother: war against the English king had begun.

King Edward's response was characteristic. He was outraged and swiftly set about a second massive campaign in Wales. He was determined 'to repress the rebellion and malice of the Welsh' and to secure the systematic annihilation of native Welsh independence. His armies spread out across Wales, seldom meeting sustained resistance. By October 1282 all of north-east Wales was captured, including Dafydd's castles and courts at Denbigh, Ruthin and Caergwrle. Whatever the nature of the defences at Denbigh, they were strong enough to withstand a month's siege by the English in the autumn of 1282.

Henry de Lacy

So it was that Denbigh fell into English hands. Immediately following the capture of the Welsh stronghold, on 16 October 1282, the campaign commander in the district, Henry de Lacy, earl of Lincoln (d. 1311), was given the *cantrefi* of Rhufoniog and Rhos, and Dinmael — a district confiscated from the rulers of northern Powys. Together they were to form a large new lordship, which took its name from its administrative centre and castle — Denbigh. During the middle fortnight of October the king was at Denbigh with Lacy, planning and setting out the

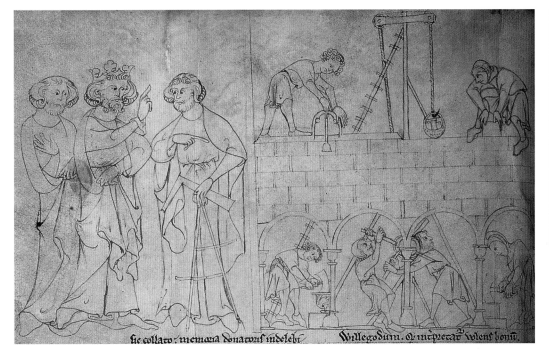

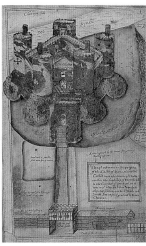

new fortifications. The presence of the king's master mason and chief building organizer, James of St George, may well indicate the king's close involvement in the siting of the castle and the plan adopted for it. Royal resources were certainly used to help with the initial operations: cartage of timber, provision of 'clays' (fencing) and purchase of tools cost £22. Once the king had started the work he left its continuation in the hands of Earl Henry.

The same pattern was repeated elsewhere on the north-east border of Wales, at Hawarden, Holt, Ruthin and Chirk. In each case, a lordship was created, a castle was designed and a baron was left to ensure its final completion. With his rear flank secured, Edward I could move against the main centre of resistance in the heart of Gwynedd and capture Llywelyn in Snowdonia. The prince, however, had left his mountainous stronghold and, as the Welsh chronicle relates, 'went to gain possession of Powys and Builth'. Here, at a place now known as Cilmeri, he met his death at the hands of an English soldier on 11 December 1282. Between January and April 1283 the castles of the Welsh princes — including Dolwyddelan, Criccieth and Castell y Bere — fell and, with the capture of the fugitive Dafydd in June 1283 followed by his gruesome public execution at Shrewsbury in October, resistance was at an end.

In March that year, construction of three royal castles had commenced in north-west Wales — Conwy, Caernarfon and Harlech — with Master James in overall charge of the works. However, unlike the full documentary record that survives for these royal castles, there is little information about the progress of work at the baronial strongholds. Nevertheless, we know that by 1284 the development of the castle and town at Denbigh was sufficiently far advanced for Lacy to be concerned with stocking his deer park. Moreover, on 1 October 1285 the earl granted the borough its first charter, which records the names of sixty-three burgesses (town dwellers who enjoyed privileges of self-government and trading concessions in return for rent, goods and services).

Top left: In this early fourteenth-century manuscript illustration, a monarch discusses building work with the supervising master mason. It is tempting to imagine a similar scene at Denbigh in October 1282 when Henry de Lacy, Edward I and James of St George may have decided upon the siting and layout of the new castle (British Library, Cotton Nero Ms. D I, f. 23v).

Above: Like Denbigh, Holt Castle, near Wrexham, was established as the centre of the new lordship of Bromfield and Yale, which the king awarded to John de Warenne, earl of Surrey (d. 1304), in October 1282. This detailed drawing of Holt was made by John Norden for a survey in 1620 (British Library, Harley Ms. 3696, f. 5).

Above left: Dafydd ap Gruffudd was captured in June 1283. Edward I regarded him as a traitor and at Shrewsbury in October of the same year he was dragged by horses to a scaffold where he was hanged, drawn and quartered (British Library, Cotton Nero Ms. D II, f. 182).

Two periods can be identified in the construction of the castle and town fortifications at Denbigh. In the first, a single, large, defensible enclosure was created by the raising of the western and southern defences of the castle and the town's walls. This work is characterized by half-round mural towers, evident to the right of this aerial view of the castle from the south. The second stage of work saw the completion of the castle's defensive circuit with the building of its northern and eastern curtain walls with polygonal towers (Skyscan Balloon Photography for Cadw).

The Progress of the Building Work

From the architectural evidence it is possible to make some definite observations about the progress of the building work. The construction of the castle and town clearly falls into two main periods. The western and southern sides of the castle were built first, with plain half-round towers and relatively thin curtain walls; the adjacent parts of the town walls on the south and west were also built at this time, shortly after 1282.

This was normal practice during the Edwardian conquest of north Wales. Wherever the lie of the land permitted such a course, a ring of outer defences was built first of all — incorporating any

pre-existing stronghold — in order to protect the workmen engaged in the building. Such workers would include diggers to excavate the ditches, quarrymen to hew the stone, masons to shape the blocks and lay them in position, carpenters to erect the floors and roofs, tilers and plumbers to cover the roofs with stone slates or lead sheets, smiths to provide the ironwork for floor nails, window and door furniture, and glaziers to install the window glass. Some of the unskilled men would be found in the earl's new lordship, but many would be recruited by royal decree as pressed labour. In the case of Denbigh, others might have been summoned from Lacy's estates in Yorkshire and Lancashire.

When this first ring of defences was complete, the next stage at Denbigh would have been to build the castle within the safety of the first enclosure, at its south-west corner. This was the highest and most easily defended part of the town. Whilst the early work, built out of limestone from the hillside, can be most easily compared with the work at Conwy, that of the second period can be likened to the magnificent castle at Caernarfon and no doubt reflects the close relationship with the royal works.

The second period of building at Denbigh saw the construction of a much thicker and higher curtain wall with internal defensive wall-passages, guarded at intervals by hexagonal or octagonal towers on the northern and eastern sides of the castle. The great gatehouse, impressively sited at the highest point of the hill, consisted of an elaborate triangular arrangement of three interconnecting octagonal towers, with a formidable entrance surmounted by a statue, perhaps representing Edward II (1307–27). It is tempting to see this design as a direct reference to the King's Gate at Caernarfon Castle and was probably planned soon after 1286; the Red Tower is also similar in plan to the wall towers at Caernarfon. The towers of the eastern wall sheltered the great hall and the private apartments of the lord and his household. The west side of the inner ward had a series of lean-to store sheds, smithies and stabling.

The second stage of the work is distinguished by a more varied choice of stone, partly for ease of working it into larger regular blocks that could be laid in ashlar courses and partly to provide finer decorative details. The main building stone is the greyish white limestone from the hilltop itself or from the outcrop north of the present town. However, this occurs in uneven beds and also weathers badly. For the great gatehouse, part of the Green Chambers, the town's Burgess Gate and the Goblin Tower, a greenish yellow fine-grained sandstone from south-west of the castle was used. These beds also provided sandstones of mottled yellows and pinks to be seen in the big eastern towers. For the Green Chambers a different sandstone, quarried at Gwespyr, 16 miles (25km) north of Denbigh, was used.

Later in the progress of the building work the distinctive red sandstone of the Triassic series was used, principally in the Red Tower and also for quoins, or angle stones, elsewhere. Another easily identified stone is the purple red sandstone used in quoins on the Red Tower, and for repairs elsewhere; its quarry was at Pontyralltgoch beside the river Elwy, some 3 miles (5km) north of Denbigh.

The second period of building at Denbigh shows many similarities to the royal work at Caernarfon Castle. Denbigh's great gatehouse, with its elaborate triangular arrangement of three interconnecting octagonal towers, may directly refer to the majestic King's Gate at Caernarfon (above). A statue of King Edward II (1307–27) was placed above the gate at Caernarfon, and it is possible that a similar figure of the ruler filled the niche on Denbigh's gatehouse (left).

Madog's Rebellion

The strength of the new defences was tested in September 1294. The Welsh, led in north Wales by Madog ap Llywelyn, a distant cousin of the last Welsh prince, rose in a widespread revolt. Although there were a number of reasons for Welsh dissatisfaction at this time, including the harsh character of the English administration, the main grievance shared by all was a particularly burdensome tax of one-fifteenth levied by the king. Several castles were captured, including those still under construction at Caernarfon and Denbigh itself. Henry de Lacy's effort to relieve the garrison failed; he was defeated and forced to retreat. In December 1294 the castle was retaken by English forces and by April 1295 the rebellion had collapsed throughout Gwynedd. As a result of the uprising, Castell y Bere in Meirionnydd (in English hands since 1283) was abandoned and a powerful new castle was built at Beaumaris to maintain a firm hold on Anglesey.

It is not clear how far castle building had progressed at Denbigh before the rebellion, but it seems likely that the major part of the eastern towers and curtain was under construction. From 1295 onwards, these were completed and the curtain wall was raised in height. The western and southern curtains (the old town wall) were also raised in height and the additional defence of the mantlet — a protective low screen wall — was erected beyond them. This enabled the construction of a second entrance to the castle — the upper gate — and an ingenious sally port, which gave the defenders a hidden exit. However, it seems likely that, when Henry de Lacy died in 1311, the great gatehouse was incomplete and may never have received the intended final storey nor any turrets.

There is a strong tradition, recorded by the antiquary, John Leland, in 1535, that the earl's eldest son, Edmund, fell to his death in the castle well; and it may have been for this reason that Henry never finished building the castle. Work was certainly still going on at the Red Tower late in the fourteenth century, but this could have been repairing decay necessitated by the use of a crumbling red sandstone. What is clear is that the principal elements of the plan were established in 1282 and that work proceeded steadily until most of it had been accomplished by 1311.

Opposite: An artist's impression of the castle and town of Denbigh as they might have looked in the early years of the fourteenth century. Following the collapse of the 1294 Welsh rebellion, led by Madog ap Llywelyn, building work continued on the town and castle, though it is unlikely that the great gatehouse ever received its intended final storey or turrets. The castle's western and southern walls were given added protection with low screen walls, or mantlets, and an upper gate was created. The salient and Goblin Tower were added at the north-eastern angle of the town walls, but, by 1305, the town had already spilled outside its defences. Although fifty-two houses stood within the walls, up to 183 were to be found outside (Illustration by Ivan Lapper, 1989).

Above: A silver penny of King Edward I, the basic unit of currency in north Wales after the English conquest.

Right: New towns, deliberately built alongside the newly established castles, were part and parcel of Edward I's plans to secure north Wales. Eager to attract English colonists, generous grants and trading privileges were offered to would-be settlers. Encouraged by the king, Henry de Lacy's first charter for the borough of Denbigh, issued in October 1285, accorded the sixty-three named burgesses what amounted to a commercial monopoly throughout the neighbourhood and numerous other attractive privileges. In return, each burgess was obliged to pay a nominal rent and to provide one armed man 'for the guard and defence' of the town (The National Archives: PRO DL 27/33).

The Castle, Town and Lordship of Denbigh

Just as Denbigh Castle provided the military support for Henry de Lacy's hold upon his new lands, so the newly founded town provided him with economic resources within his lordship. Indeed, new town 'plantations' were part and parcel of the Edwardian military settlement in Wales and contributed in no small way to its initial and sustained success.

Towns had been few and far between in Wales before the Norman conquest; cattle not coinage was the main unit of exchange. Until the Normans established Rhuddlan at the mouth of the Clwyd in 1073 — with castle, borough and mint — the nearest town had been at Chester. In the north at least, the pattern changed little over the next 200 years, though in the late twelfth century it is likely that the newly established cathedral at St Asaph had a town laid out beside it. Around 1250 Degannwy, beside the river Conwy, had a new town situated

below the castle, which was held briefly by the English between 1245 and 1262. By this time, too, it should be said that urban centres — albeit small ones — were also appearing in native Wales.

Yet, despite these developments, the fresh start made at Rhuddlan in 1277, and the new towns at Denbigh and Ruthin following King Edward I's conquest of 1282–83, represent something quite new. Both east and west of the river Conwy, the Edwardian planned boroughs mark an urban growth which was never again to wither away.

The towns were conceived as a whole and, in each case, the planning, layout and construction went hand in hand with work on the castle. At Caernarfon and Conwy, as at Denbigh, the town walls were integrated with those of the castle itself. Each castle garrison needed the market traders to provide them with supplies and luxuries. Each town community needed the defensive walls and the garrison's protection when the local Welsh were hostile. Moreover, with the castle's constable dominating the borough, he would see that the townsfolk met their premier obligation to defend the ramparts in time of need.

Throughout north Wales, the town was used by the king and his supporters as a prime instrument for establishing an effective English civilian presence in the new province. Colonists were encouraged to settle in the fledgling towns by a series of very favourable grants and trading privileges. At Denbigh, in particular, the settler families enjoyed a commercial monopoly throughout the neighbourhood. Some families also held profitable lands within the new lordship, outside the immediate confines of the borough.

In addition to such policies in the boroughs, the Edwardian military conquest meant that the Welsh countryside, too, was to see significant social and economic change. Once more, the new lordship created around the castle and borough at Denbigh demonstrates just how remarkable the changes could be.

Encouraged by new land-owning opportunities, English peasant settlers were attracted to Denbigh in large numbers. Many thousands of acres of land, especially around the castle-borough and in the Vale of Clwyd, were transferred from native Welshmen to the land-hungry immigrants. The displaced Welsh were sometimes compensated, but often with lands in remote and infertile upland districts.

For Henry de Lacy, of course, the motives for these changes were not only military and political control; there were also considerable economic advantages. The borough at Denbigh, as the centre of the extensive lordship, provided the headquarters for the clerks needed by the earl to administer it. It also housed the steward and various officials he required to maintain law and order there, and the financial officers he employed to raise revenues from the lordship.

Many of these English settlers, both in borough and countryside, would have come from Lacy's lands in Lancashire or Yorkshire, where Pontefract was the centre of a similar lordship with a flourishing market town and trading centre near the river Aire. Others may have been tempted from Cheshire and the border by the various housing, trading or land rights and privileges.

It is hardly surprising that the groundswell of native resentment against these harsh changes grew. In despair, the Welsh rose in spasmodic outbursts of violence throughout the lordship in the fourteenth century. This frequently left the burgesses of the

town in a terrified state, and led in no small part to the prominence of Welshmen from the lordship of Denbigh in the Glyn Dŵr revolt in the early years of the next century (p. 14).

Lancaster and Mortimer

On the death of Henry de Lacy in 1311 without a male heir, the castle passed to his elder daughter, Alice. She was married to Thomas, earl of Lancaster (d. 1322), and so became embroiled in the political unrest of Edward II's reign. Her marriage, none the less, ensured that both castle and town came into the hands of a great magnate, well able to continue the necessary building work, both here at Denbigh and at Pontefract. Indeed, progress with the building work, albeit slow, seems to have continued at Denbigh until

Top: Just as at Conwy, seen here in an aerial view, the castle and borough at Denbigh were planned and built as an integrated whole.

Above: The centre of Henry de Lacy's lordship in Yorkshire was Pontefract, where his great castle — depicted here by the early seventeenth-century artist, Alexander Keirincx (d. 1652) — overlooked a prosperous market town. Some of the English settlers who came to the lordship of Denbigh may have come from Lacy's lands in Yorkshire or Lancashire (© Wakefield Museums and Galleries, West Yorkshire / The Bridgeman Art Library).

Roger Mortimer (d. 1360) was created second earl of March in 1354 and recovered Denbigh in the following year; the castle and lordship would remain in the hands of the Mortimers until 1425. Roger was one of the founding members of the Order of the Garter, and is depicted in his Garter robes in this fifteenth-century manuscript illustration from the Bruges Garter Book *(British Library, Stowe Ms. 594, f. 15v).*

the execution of Earl Thomas, on a charge of treason, at his own castle of Pontefract in 1322.

After his death, the lordship of Denbigh seems to have been regarded by the king as a suitable prize to be awarded for loyal support. It was held first by Hugh Despenser, earl of Winchester, a favoured courtier of Edward II. Following Despenser's execution in 1326 and the king's murder in 1327, it passed to Roger Mortimer, earl of March (d. 1330). Then in 1330, after Queen Isabella (Edward II's widow) had been captured with her favourite, Mortimer, it was granted to William Montagu (d. 1344) — later earl of Salisbury — who held it for twelve years until his death. Eventually, the Mortimer earls of March regained Denbigh in 1355 and the lordship formed an important outlier of their estates, based on the central Marches of the Herefordshire-Shropshire border, until the death of the last Mortimer heir, Edmund, in 1425.

During the first half of the fourteenth century, it is likely that building work continued on the Red Tower, the mantlet and its gates, the Countess Tower, the Goblin Tower and the salient, together with the inner walls of the two town gatehouses. The internal ranges of the castle were also completed at this time, though work was still in progress late in the century for the earls of March.

In 1374, a sum of £21 was spent on roofing material for the Red Tower, and on other minor repairs in stone and timber. In 1398 and again in 1411–12 — both occasions when the castle was in royal hands — there are accounts for work at the

Red Tower, the 'Green Tower' (probably the White Chamber Tower) and at the 'New Tower' (perhaps the lower gate of the castle postern or the Goblin Tower on the town defences). Most of these financial accounts relate to minor repairs caused by rotting timber or crumbling sandstone.

In September 1400 the town of Denbigh was one of the targets of the first raid of Owain Glyn Dŵr, who led the revolt that encompassed much of Wales during the first decade of the fifteenth century. The burgesses no doubt fled for safety to the castle. The rebellion was brought about, yet again, by excessive taxation and the insensitivity of English officials, though there was the added friction of a personal quarrel between Owain and his close neighbour, Reginald Grey of Ruthin and Dyffryn Clwyd. During the next two and a half years Denbigh and its castle were held on behalf of King Henry IV (1399–1413) by Henry Percy (d. 1403), better known as Hotspur, the son of the first earl of Northumberland (d. 1408). His task was a daunting one as the tide of rebellion swept across Wales in 1402–03. In 1403 Hotspur defected from the king's side and conspired with Glyn Dŵr. It was a serious blow to the rebel cause when Percy was defeated and killed on 21 July in that same year at the Battle of Shrewsbury. Life must have been precarious for the garrison at Denbigh in the succeeding years, but we have no record that the castle fell. It is probable that Glyn Dŵr spared the lordship of Denbigh because it was the inheritance of Edmund Mortimer (d. 1425), heir apparent to the earldom of March, whose uncle — following his capture by the Welsh in 1402 — had very quickly made alliance with Owain and married his daughter, Catherine. In 1405 the young Mortimer was brought into a scheme whereby England and Wales would be divided into three parts shared between Glyn Dŵr (west), Mortimer (central and south), and Henry Percy, earl of Northumberland (mainly north). This scheme remained a dream after Northumberland was defeated in battle and Mortimer was recaptured after his escape from Windsor Castle in February 1405. By May 1407 the rebellion was practically over and Denbigh was free from danger. The principal targets of the rebels were rebuilt: the courthouse and the lord's mills. Heavy communal and individual fines were levied and, more ominously, new chests were ordered for the collection of tolls exacted from tenants bringing their corn to the mills.

Henry Percy, Keeper of the Lordship of Denbigh

Above: The great seal of Owain Glyn Dŵr, who led the revolt that threw much of Wales into turmoil during the first decade of the fifteenth century. Denbigh was threatened in September 1400 in the course of Glyn Dŵr's first raid, but he may have spared the lordship in the latter stages of the uprising because of the close alliance he had forged with the Mortimer family in 1402. (National Museum of Wales).

Left: Sir Henry Percy — better known as 'Hotspur' — was the eldest son of the earl of Northumberland. His support for King Henry IV was rewarded with important appointments, including keeper of the lordship of Denbigh. Percy was responsible for the defence of Denbigh in the early stages of the Glyn Dŵr uprising, but his growing discontent with the Crown led him to intrigue with the Welsh leader in 1403 and to raise the standard of revolt. He died on 21 July 1403 in the fierce fighting at the Battle of Shrewsbury, which is vividly portrayed in this illustration from the late fifteenth-century Beauchamp Pageants (British Library, Cotton Julius Ms. E IV, art. 6, f. 4).

At the outbreak of the Glyn Dŵr revolt in September 1400, Edmund Mortimer, heir of Denbigh and later earl of March, was a minor, and since 1398 the lordship had been in royal custody. Henry IV appointed Henry Percy as keeper of the lordship of Denbigh, as well as justiciar of Chester and north Wales, in charge of all aspects of royal administration in the region. The celebrated Percy, more familiar to readers of Shakespeare as 'this Hotspur Mars in swathing clothes, this infant warrior (*Henry IV, Part 1*, Act III, Scene II), was at Denbigh in person in June 1402, and doubtless stayed at the castle. The following year, his growing discontent with the Crown led him to enter into negotiations with Glyn Dŵr.

In April 1403, one of Hotspur's squires, William Lloyd of Denbigh, travelled to Berwick (Northumberland). Young William's mission was to confer with his master, and he was almost certainly carrying the threads of an intrigue direct from the Welsh leader. Hotspur clearly wished to count on Glyn Dŵr's support when he raised the standard of rebellion. But it was all to no avail since Hotspur was killed at the Battle of Shrewsbury on 21 July 1403.

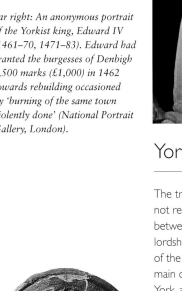

The seal of Jasper Tudor, earl of Pembroke (d. 1495). Unable to occupy the castle and take up his post of constable, Jasper twice launched attacks on Denbigh. He secured it briefly in 1460, but in 1468 only succeeded in burning the town within the walls (British Library).

York and Tudor

The troubled state of affairs in the early 1400s was not resolved during the Wars of the Roses (1455–85) between the houses of Lancaster and York. The lordship of Denbigh, which had long been in the hands of the Mortimer family, was to become one of the main centres of support for their heirs, the dukes of York, and the Yorkist cause in Wales. The Lancastrian King Henry VI (1422–61, 1470–71), however, appointed his half-brother Jasper Tudor, earl of Pembroke (d. 1495), to the post of constable — or governor — of Denbigh Castle in 1457. This was an empty gesture until Jasper could actually occupy the castle.

On two occasions Jasper did launch determined attacks on Denbigh; he held it for a few months in 1460, just before the death of Richard, duke of York, at the Battle of Wakefield at the end of the year. But soon after York's son, Edward (later King Edward IV, 1461–70, 1471–83), was successful at the Battle of Towton. On his second attempt, in 1468, Jasper Tudor failed to take the castle, but burned the town within the walls.

It was claimed that, because of this disaster, the townsfolk moved away from the hilltop defences, and established a new town on the lower ground where the present marketplace is situated. The cellars under

some of the shops may date from this move, though the arcades that support the houses over those shops are probably of the late Tudor or early Stuart period.

When it was first built the castle needed the town as an added protection, but now, 200 years later, the townsfolk did not wish to be a prime target as they shielded the castle. After the 1468 attack, Thomas Stringer was appointed 'porter of the gate of the outer ward of [the King's] castle of Denbigh and surveyor of his works there', a title which suggests that the town gate (probably the Exchequer Gate) was seen as part of the castle. The last echo of these wars seems to be the grant of 200 marks (£133) for the repair of the town walls early in 1485, being the balance of 1,500 marks (£1,000) granted by the Yorkist king, Edward IV, in 1462 to the burgesses of Denbigh towards rebuilding 'by occasion of burning of the same town violently done'.

During the sixteenth century little was done beyond carrying out some routine maintenance under Robert Lloyd who was described as 'clerk of the works and repairs'. Under the Tudors, particularly Henry VIII (1509–47) and Elizabeth I (1558–1603), there were regular surveys made to assess costs of repair and to determine whether, in time of peace, these castles were necessary to the Crown, or whether they should be sold or demolished to save the costs.

The Layout and Extent of the Town

Protected by its walls, the town gave economic support to the military garrison in the castle. When the borough was originally laid out some sixty-three burgesses each held an individual burgage plot, and there was an attempt to lay out these properties within the regular street plan. By 1305, however, the town had already expanded beyond the walls, with just fifty-two houses within the defences and up to 183 outside.

The inconvenience of the hilltop site, the irregular water supply, and the cramped space for market activities meant that the extramural settlement continued to grow. Despite the setbacks of the fifteenth century, in 1476 there were still sixty-five burgages within the walls. But the town as a whole had spread far more onto the flatter ground, where there were 276 burgages, in the area now represented by the streets around the marketplace and, later, Lord Leicester's new town hall of 1571.

In 1586 the antiquarian and historian, William Camden (d. 1623), observed: 'The old town is now deserted and a new one, much larger, sprung up at the foot of the hill which is now so populous that the church not being large enough for the inhabitants, they have now begun to build a new one where the old town stood'. By the time of the Civil War (1642–48) only a few houses remained within the walls and this area was regarded as the outer ward of the castle (p. 20).

The first common seal of the burgesses of Denbigh, which was appended to Henry de Lacy's copy of the borough charter in 1285 (The National Archives: PRO DL 27/33).

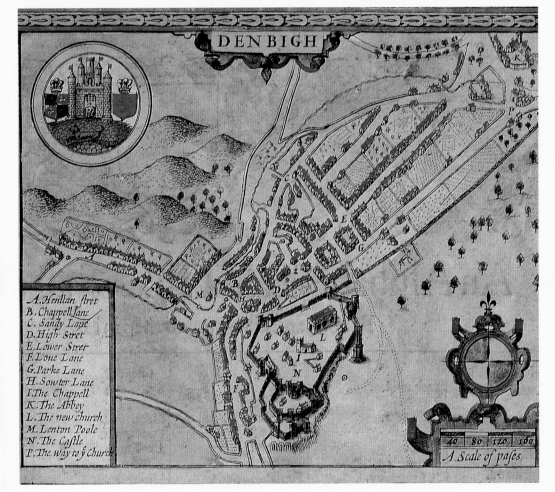

A. Henllan Stret
B. Chappell Lane
C. Sandy Lane
D. High Stret
E. Lower Stret
F. Loue Lane
G. Parke Lane
H. Sowter Lane
I. The Chappell
K. The Abbey
L. The new church
M. Lenton Poole
N. The Castle
P. The way to ƴ Church

This 1610 map of Denbigh by John Speed confirms William Camden's report of twenty years earlier that the 'old town' within the walls had been deserted and that the community was flourishing on the flatter ground at the base of the hill. St Hilary's Chapel (I) and Lord Leicester's great new church (L) are clearly visible. In the upper right hand corner of the map, Denbigh Friary (K) is also shown (National Library of Wales).

Right: A page from the detailed survey of the castle made in 1561, which revealed that much of the castle was ruinous or in utter decay. The names of many of the towers and lodgings in the castle are only known from this survey (The National Archives: PRO SC 12/27/28, f. 3).

Far right: Elizabeth I's dashing favourite, Robert Dudley (d. 1588), in an anonymous portrait painted about 1575. Dudley was granted the castle and lordship of Denbigh in 1563, and a year later he was created Baron Denbigh and earl of Leicester. He used his position to become the virtual governor-general of north Wales. (National Portrait Gallery, London).

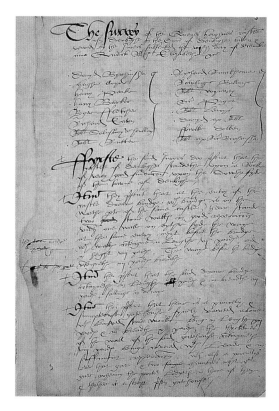

Above: The cathedral church at St Asaph, which Robert Dudley may have hoped to replace with the splendid new church that he began to construct at Denbigh in 1578. The earl of Leicester also built a new market hall in Denbigh and undertook some repairs to the castle and town walls.

One survey of Denbigh, taken in about 1530, described the great gatehouse as capable of being repaired at little charge; the Green Chambers and the Treasure House Tower were well repaired; 'all the rest are much in decay in the timberwork, and most in the lead'. In 1532 the bishop of St Asaph was using one of the towers as the prison of his diocese.

The recognition of Denbigh as the centre of one of the shires, newly created in 1536, meant that the castle had a revival of fortunes: a courthouse, record office, prison and judges' lodging would be needed. Those parts of the castle which could fulfil these functions would be maintained. Here, as at so many other former baronial castles now in royal hands, it was their function as court and prison rather than an active military role that gave them a new lease of life in the sixteenth century.

In 1561 a full and detailed survey was made of the castle. This showed that only the great gatehouse, Great Kitchen Tower, Treasure House Tower, Red Tower and the Green Chambers were in good repair; the rest of the buildings were either ruinous or in utter decay. In fact it is from this survey that the names of many of the towers and lodgings are known.

Denbigh under Lord Leicester

The continuing upkeep of so many Welsh castles in time of peace dismayed Elizabeth I's councillors, and they tried to shift the burden by granting out such castles on a repairing lease. In 1563 Robert Dudley (d. 1588), who was the favourite companion of the queen, was granted the castle and lordship of Denbigh and a year later he was created Baron Denbigh and earl of Leicester. He became virtually governor-general of north Wales. He used both the Star Chamber and the Council in the Marches of Wales as instruments of his overbearing control, acting through the Sidney family as his main agents. The constables of the castle were successive members of the Middleton family of Galch Hill.

Leicester undertook some small repairs to the residential parts of the castle and to the town walls, and also built a new market hall in 1571. His greatest effort, however, went into the large new church which he erected inside the walls in 1578. Leicester may have intended this church to replace St Asaph as the cathedral for north-east Wales.

The Civil War 1642–48

At his death, the earl of Leicester had left the castle in a state little better than when he received it from Queen Elizabeth I. Two further surveys in 1594 and 1603 indicated that the habitable parts of the castle were restricted to the Green Chambers and the four large towers (Red Tower, the great gatehouse, Great Kitchen Tower and White Chamber Tower). The other towers and walls, both of the castle and of the town — the latter now regarded as the outer ward of the castle — were in decay and beyond repair.

As late as 1621 only part of the castle was habitable by its governor. Following the outbreak of civil war between king and parliament in 1642, the task of making Denbigh a fully defensible refuge for a royalist garrison of 500 men was a massive undertaking. Colonel William Salesbury (d.1660) of Rug near Corwen (a distant branch of the Salusburys of Lleweni, patrons of the white friars at Denbigh) was responsible for Denbigh Castle. From the time of his appointment in 1643 the colonel spent liberally from his estates in the king's cause. His neighbour, Archbishop John Williams (d. 1650), did likewise in

fortifying Conwy Castle, and other loyal gentry families and clergy contributed.

The main course of the Civil War was fought in central and northern England, with only a few skirmishes in Wales and the borders, as marauding bands of cavalry sought to harass the supply lines of their opponents. Nevertheless, defeats at Marston Moor, near York, in July 1644 and at Naseby, near Northampton, in June 1645 put royalist Wales in danger from parliamentary armies. Later the same year, King Charles I (1625–49) attempted to lift the siege of Chester but his forces were defeated at Rowton Heath, south of the city, on 24 September 1645. The king then retreated to Denbigh and stayed there for three nights. Traditionally, he is believed to have lodged in the Great Kitchen Tower, afterwards known to Victorian antiquaries as the King's Chamber or King Charles's Tower.

Another royalist force of 2,000 men led by Sir William Vaughan hoped to relieve Chester and assembled at Denbigh Green on 31 October 1645. The following day they were attacked by a larger parliamentary force led by Sir William Brereton (d. 1661) and Sir Thomas Mytton (d. 1656) and were utterly routed in the fields around Denbigh Friary.

Far left: Archbishop John Williams (d. 1650), who used his personal fortune to fortify and garrison neighbouring Conwy Castle in support of the royalist cause during the Civil War. Colonel William Salesbury (d. 1660) undertook a similar commitment at Denbigh (Ashmolean Museum, Oxford).

Left: Sir Thomas Mytton (d. 1656) was one of parliament's most important commanders in north Wales during the Civil War. He was in joint command of a force that routed a royalist army of 2,000 men at Denbigh Green on 1 November 1645 and in April of the next year he laid siege to the town and castle of Denbigh. This contemporary print appeared in 1647 in John Vicars's England's Worthies *(British Library).*

Right: A view of the Goblin Tower on Denbigh's town walls from one of the earthwork bastions that the parliamentary forces threw up to protect their siege guns. The besiegers concentrated their main efforts on the Goblin Tower, which protected the defenders' only reliable source of water. The garrison of 500 men held out for six months, before, disappointed in all hopes of relief, they resigned themselves to surrender on honourable terms.

Above: This illustration from an early seventeenth-century treatise on artillery (Johann Jacobi, Archiley Kriegskunst) shows a cannon similar to those used by the besiegers to batter Denbigh's defences in 1646 (British Library).

Right: George Monck, first duke of Albermarle (d. 1670), issued the orders for the slighting of Denbigh Castle in March 1660. During the ensuing demolition work, which lasted six weeks, two towers were pulled down and the castle's curtain walls were breached to make the stronghold indefensible (National Portrait Gallery, London).

One hundred men were killed, 400 captured and many of the injured took refuge in Denbigh Castle. The remainder fled to the safety of Conwy Castle.

Although some English towns were quite closely encircled by siege lines dug by the parliamentary attackers, the castle sieges were more 'leisurely' affairs, occasionally embittered by local family feuds when captives were shot. Colonel Salesbury withstood a six-month siege from April to October 1646. He was then aged 66 and affectionately known to his men as 'Hen Hosannau Gleision' (Old Blue Stockings). Though called on to surrender at least five times by the parliamentary commander, Sir Thomas Mytton, he replied that he had vowed to serve the king loyally and would only surrender Denbigh at the king's written command. Throughout the siege, both the castle and the town walls were held as one. The main efforts of the attackers were directed at an attempt to batter down the Goblin Tower and so deprive the garrison of its only reliable water supply in the height of summer. Below this tower, on level ground (now the school playing fields), the parliamentary forces dug crescent-shaped earthwork bastions, or 'half-moons', to protect their artillery. Other guns were placed on Galch Hill to break down the thinner mantlet and curtain wall on the south-west side. In response, the castle had only one gun to defend it.

However, it was the isolation of this 500-man garrison from all hope of relief that brought about its surrender on honourable terms. On 26 October they marched out with flags flying, drums beating, trumpets sounding and firearms loaded. For the remainder of the war the castle was used as a prison for captured royalists, and during the Commonwealth and Protectorate — the period between 1649 and 1660 when the country was ruled solely by parliament — a small garrison was based there. In 1659, a band of royalist troops successfully retook the castle for a brief period and thus sealed the fate of what had been an impregnable medieval fortress. In March 1660, the castle was slighted (made indefensible) on the orders of General Monck (d. 1670); demolition took six weeks and concentrated on breaking down the curtain walls and pulling down two major towers.

William Salesbury of Rug and Bachymbyd

William Salesbury (1580–1660) came from a Welsh landowning family with an estate near Corwen and a house near Denbigh. After studying at Oxford, he spent time as a pikeman fighting for the Protestants in the Netherlands and as a privateer in the East Indies. When he inherited his estates in 1611 he took on the role of a country gentleman, serving briefly as a Member of Parliament in 1620–21. He wrote religious poetry in Welsh and encouraged a Welsh translation of William Brough's *Manual of Prayer*. He built a private chapel at Rug in 1637, which is extensively decorated with religious imagery.

William Salesbury served Charles I faithfully as governor of Denbigh Castle, speaking plainly to the king when he stayed in September 1645 — so honestly that the king remarked: 'Never did a prince hear so much truth at once'. On the eve of the king's execution in 1649, Charles sent Salesbury an embroidered cap of crimson silk as a token of his respect for him. During the Commonwealth and Protectorate (1649–60), Salesbury was heavily fined for his tenacious loyalty and then lived 'in obscurity and comparative indigence'. Perhaps in the siege and later life he was sustained by his family motto: *A vynno Dew dervid* (What God wills will come to pass). He was buried at Llanynys near Denbigh.

Above: William Salesbury of Rug (d. 1660), the defender of Denbigh, was affectionately known by his men as 'Hen Hosannau Gleision' (Old Blue Stockings) (By kind permission of Nancy, Lady Bagot).

Far left: Salesbury's private chapel at Rug was constructed in 1637.

Left: The triple portrait of King Charles I (1625–49) by Anthony Van Dyck (d. 1661). Charles stayed at Denbigh for three nights after his forces were defeated at Rowton Heath near Chester in 1645 (The Royal Collection © 2006, Her Majesty Queen Elizabeth II).

Later History

After the restoration of King Charles II (1660–85) the castle and town walls were allowed to fall into ruin and became a ready source of house-building material. In the eighteenth century the ruins of the castle and town were depicted by engravers like the Buck brothers in 1742, and John Boydell (d. 1804) of Hawarden in 1750. Later in the century, the historian, Thomas Pennant (d. 1798), sent his artist, Moses Griffith (d. 1819), to illustrate Denbigh for *The Journey to Snowdonia*, but this castle was a less popular subject than the Romantic ruins of Conwy or Harlech, or the Welsh stronghold of Dolbadarn.

In the mid-nineteenth century, spurred on by civic pride, a 'Castle Committee' was formed to keep the ruins in repair, and considerable clearance work was carried out. In 1914, the castle and town walls were vested in H. M. Office of Works. They are now maintained by Cadw, the Welsh Assembly Government's historic environment service, as are Denbigh Friary, St Hilary's Chapel and Lord Leicester's Church.

Left: Denbigh was a less popular subject for artists than the more Romantic ruins at Conwy, Harlech and Dolbadarn. However, this engraving, published in 1750 by John Boydell of nearby Hawarden, provides a detailed view of the town and castle from the north. The twin-towered Burgess Gate stands out prominently on the town walls, and Lord Leicester's church is already derelict and roofless. The damage done to the castle by the slighting after the Civil War siege and later stone robbing is evident (National Library of Wales).

Below: A 'Castle Committee' had been founded in the mid-nineteenth century to keep the ruins in repair, and by the time this photograph of the great gatehouse was taken near the end of the century considerable clearance work had been carried out.

A Tour of Denbigh Castle

The tour suggests one route around the interior of the castle and describes the principal features of interest. It is not intended to be rigid and visitors may investigate the various parts of the castle in any order using the bird's-eye view (inside front cover) or the ground plan (inside back cover) as a guide. Our route, however, begins at the main entrance — the great gatehouse — guides you around the interior clockwise, visiting each tower in turn, and brings you back to where you started. When you leave the castle, you can turn left for the circuit of the town walls ending at this same point.

If time is limited, however, visitors may care to go directly to St Hilary's Chapel, Lord Leicester's Church and the best preserved stretch of the town walls — from the Burgess Gate to the Goblin Tower. Access to the town walls should be arranged via the custodian at the castle or keys may be borrowed from the library in High Street.

From the level gravel car park a firm path gently climbs to the gatehouse where a sloping timber bridge leads into the castle. There is level access to the visitor centre. The ward is mainly grass. There are some steep areas but much can be seen from level areas.

Stone steps give access to the wall-walks, towers and the Green Chambers. Some flights are spiral and some have no handrails.

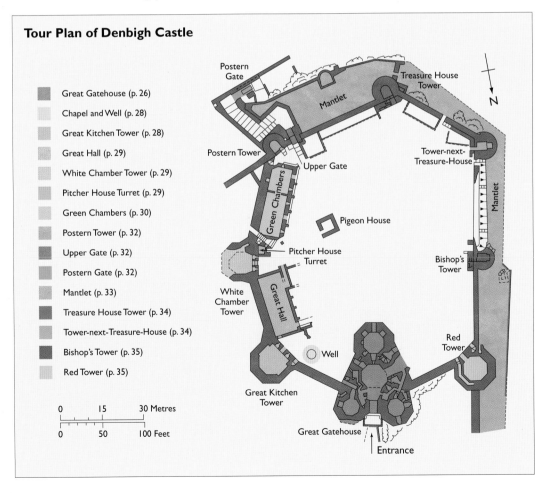

Tour Plan of Denbigh Castle

- Great Gatehouse (p. 26)
- Chapel and Well (p. 28)
- Great Kitchen Tower (p. 28)
- Great Hall (p. 29)
- White Chamber Tower (p. 29)
- Pitcher House Turret (p. 29)
- Green Chambers (p. 30)
- Postern Tower (p. 32)
- Upper Gate (p. 32)
- Postern Gate (p. 32)
- Mantlet (p. 33)
- Treasure House Tower (p. 34)
- Tower-next-Treasure-House (p. 34)
- Bishop's Tower (p. 35)
- Red Tower (p. 35)

0   15   30 Metres
0   50   100 Feet

Postern Gate
Treasure House Tower
Mantlet
Postern Tower
Tower-next-Treasure-House
Upper Gate
Green Chambers
Mantlet
Pigeon House
Pitcher House Turret
Bishop's Tower
White Chamber Tower
Great Hall
Red Tower
Well
Great Kitchen Tower
Great Gatehouse
Entrance
N

Opposite: Even in its ruined state, the grandeur of Denbigh Castle's great gatehouse is unmistakable. Standing on the highest point of the castle hill, it was undoubtedly intended to proclaim authority as well as military strength. It is noteworthy that octagonal towers, banded masonry and a regal statue are found together elsewhere only at the royal castle of Caernarfon. The original plans for the gatehouse may have included another storey and turrets, but these were probably never completed.

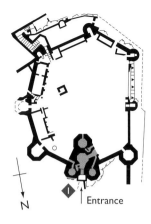

N   ◆ I   Entrance

The Plan of the Castle

In plan, the castle walls appear as a great oval enclosing an inner ward. There is a contrast between the early work on the west and south walls and the later work on the north and east. The early work consists of straight lines of walls connecting now poorly surviving semicircular towers, whereas the later work is characterized by short lengths of wall that connect the better-preserved polygonal towers, with many courtyard buildings set between them.

Beyond the castle, to the south, is an elaborate additional defensive line of walls, towers and gates; this protective line or 'mantlet' also survives on the west, where the early work was not as strong as the great polygonal towers and tall curtain walls.

Great Gatehouse

This main entrance to the castle was the most impressive of all the Edwardian works at Denbigh, and received a high degree of architectural decoration. First, there was a barbican, or outer passage, on the far side of the castle ditch with its own entrance gateway. From here, a drawbridge crossed the ditch into the great gatehouse, which consists of three octagonal towers, one on either side of the entrance and the third behind them within the courtyard. The main entrance itself was an impressive arch with a decorated niche above containing a statue of a seated man, probably King Edward II. It is noteworthy that Denbigh and Caernarfon are the only castles designed with

An artist's impression of the great gatehouse with the Porter's Lodge Tower cut away to show the formidable defences of the gate-passage and other internal arrangements. (Illustration by Chris Jones-Jenkins, 1990).

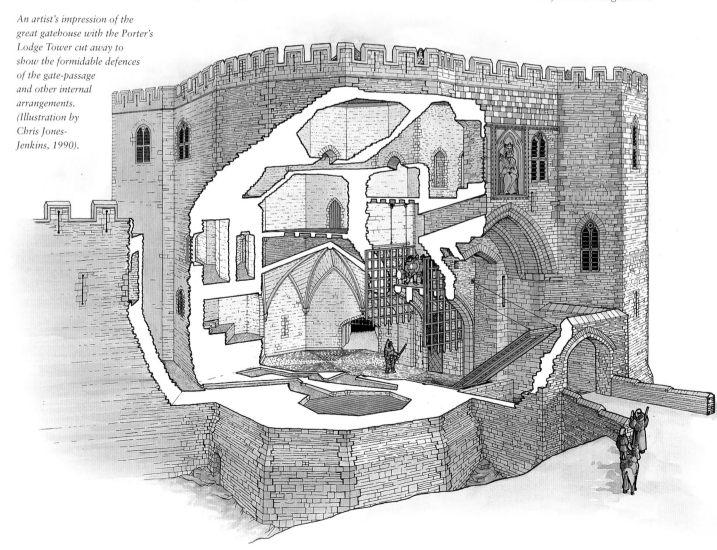

octagonal towers, colour-banded masonry and royal statues over the entrances. The symbolism of this combination should not be overlooked. Although we cannot be certain of all its meanings, no doubt authority was intended: Denbigh had replaced the main castle of Dafydd ap Gruffudd and Caernarfon became the centre of Edward I's administration in north Wales, which displaced the authority of Llywelyn ap Gruffudd.

These three towers and their connecting walls enclosed a large central hall. To reach this hall, friend and foe alike had to pass along a strongly defended passage (**A** on marginal plan) beneath two 'murder holes' in the roof vault, through which defenders could drop missiles, and past a portcullis. They were then confronted by a door that opened outwards and was protected by arrowloops in the side walls. Ahead, the way could be barred by a second portcullis. Just beyond this, a door on the left led into the porter's lodge.

The octagonal hall (**B** on marginal plan) was impressively vaulted in stone. Above the vault there was a storage space, with corbels to support the floor of the octagonal room over it. Another room was certainly planned above this, but it may never have been completed.

The inner entry (**C** on marginal plan) was guarded by a portcullis and a double-leaf door. The position of the portcullis is shown by the grooves through which it was raised and lowered, and the position of the doorway is indicated by drawbar holes, where a strong timber beam was slid across the rear of the door. The portcullis mechanisms were housed in the rooms immediately above the entry passages, and these rooms acted as the link between the three towers of the great gatehouse.

The tower on the right (west) of the inner entrance, just before you reach the inner ward, was the Prison Tower. A vaulted passage, set diagonally in the wall thickness, led directly to the ground-floor room. To the right of the passage were two small rooms, separated by a deep window embrasure, which was used in the defence of the two entrances to the gatehouse. To the left of the passage there were latrines with five different chutes discharging into a common cesspit. The main ground-floor room was a prison chamber, and below it there was a deep vaulted windowless prison; its only ventilation was an air hole in the north-east wall. Originally, it was

accessible only by a trapdoor; the steps are Victorian in date and were built for visitors to the castle.

The other two towers were similar in plan to the Prison Tower. Both were approached at ground level from within the courtyard. Badnes Tower, to the left of the inner entry, may take its name from an early constable of the castle. It has a basement and three storeys, and the ground-floor room shows a high standard of comfort with a fireplace, a latrine and three windows. The Porter's Lodge Tower is now badly ruined but seems to have been much plainer in its internal arrangements; it did not have a basement.

The upper floors of the gatehouse are approached by a stair just beyond and to the left (south) of the inner entrance. It was well protected by two successive doors, which led to a circular stair to reach two of the towers, and a straight stair giving access to the Porter's Lodge Tower. The principal consideration in planning was to combine privacy with the needs of defence. The four main rooms on the first and second floors were self-contained, ensuring privacy for their occupants. Passages enabled defenders to reach the portcullis chambers and to move quickly to the tops of the towers, as well as to

The central hall of the gatehouse has lost the impressive ribbed vault that once covered the octagonal space. A low storage space was sandwiched between the vault and the floor of the room above, which was supported on corbels. Another room was planned above, but it may never have been built.

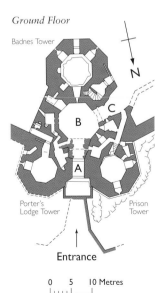

Ground Floor

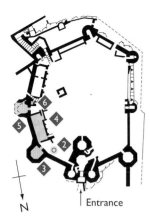

Right: The rear of the great gatehouse viewed from the inner ward. The large opening visible on the left marks the end of the passage that gave access from the gatehouse's central hall to the interior of the castle. It was guarded with a portcullis and a double-leaf door. The Badnes Tower, which may have acquired its name from an early constable of the castle, stands to the right. Like the other towers of the gatehouse, it contained comfortable apartments and was well provided with latrines.

According to a tradition recorded in 1535 by the Tudor antiquary, John Leland, Henry de Lacy's eldest son, Edmund, died when he fell into the castle well.

climb up to the wall-walks between these towers. All of the towers were well provided with latrines, usually lit by narrow rectangular windows. The wall-walk from the great gatehouse to the Great Kitchen Tower was originally a passage in the thickness of the wall, similar to those that can still be seen at Caernarfon and Beaumaris. On the left are embrasures that were probably provided with arrowloops. Above this passage was a second walk at a higher level, on top of the curtain wall. Both walks led to the stair in the Great Kitchen Tower and were the first and highest stretch of a continuous defensive walk to be built around the entire curtain wall of the castle.

Chapel and Well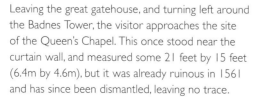

Leaving the great gatehouse, and turning left around the Badnes Tower, the visitor approaches the site of the Queen's Chapel. This once stood near the curtain wall, and measured some 21 feet by 15 feet (6.4m by 4.6m), but it was already ruinous in 1561 and has since been dismantled, leaving no trace.

A second chapel stood on the opposite side of the courtyard — near the Bishop's Tower — but this has also been demolished.

Close to the Great Kitchen Tower is the castle well, which is over 50 feet (15.2m) deep. It was here that Edmund de Lacy, the eldest son of the castle's builder, Henry de Lacy, is reputed to have fallen to his death. One other free-standing medieval building in the courtyard was the pigeon house, the foundations of which stand near the Green Chambers.

Great Kitchen Tower

This tower, on the east curtain wall, was an irregular hexagon that stood three storeys high. It can now only be entered at courtyard level, but there is a good view of it from the wall-walk leading from the great gatehouse. Its main features are the two great fireplaces, each 16 feet wide (4.9m), set in the north and south walls of the ground floor. These fireplaces are probably alterations of a later period as they require ingenious flue passages to carry the smoke past the existing upper windows. There have also been many alterations on the first floor, shown by the way in which the windows have been blocked and red sandstone used for repairs.

The upper floors were reached directly from the courtyard by a stair, the remains of which can be seen on the north-west corner of the tower. At second-floor level a wall-passage linked the two defensive wall-walks to the great gatehouse with the single wall-walk to the White Chamber Tower.

Great Hall

South of the Great Kitchen Tower are the foundations of the great hall. A buttery and pantry stood against the face of the Great Kitchen Tower, and from them a door led into the screens passage of the hall. A porch gave entry to the hall from the courtyard. Some idea of the height and decoration of the hall is given by the two corbels surviving out of the ten originally placed in the curtain wall. The south-west porch at the other end of the hall led from beside the dais into the lord's private apartments situated in the White Chamber Tower and the Green Chambers.

White Chamber Tower 5

This tower has suffered badly from the effects of Civil War slighting. It originally stood three storeys high and would have looked like the Great Kitchen Tower. The basement was reached by a flight of steps down from the courtyard and was lit by two small windows either side of the doorway. The upper floors were reached by a circular stair in the south-west corner (now fallen into the Green Chambers). These upper rooms provided attractive accommodation: they were well lit and each was provided with a fireplace and latrine.

The tower overlooks the bowling green, which can be viewed from the car park outside the castle.

Pitcher House Turret 6

Between the White Chamber Tower and the north wall of the Green Chambers is the base of a small square turret and a broad flight of steps descending to a postern gate (now blocked) in the curtain wall.

Left: The upper floors of the Great Kitchen Tower were reached directly by a stair from the courtyard. Inside, the main features are the two enormous fireplaces that seem to have been inserted as alterations into the ground floor of the tower at a later date. According to tradition, King Charles I was accommodated in this tower during his stay at Denbigh in 1645.

Below left: This marginal illustration from the fourteenth-century Luttrell Psalter shows cooks roasting fowl and a piglet on a spit. The fireplaces in the Great Kitchen Tower would have been well suited to cooking food in this way (British Library, Additional Ms. 42130, f. 206v).

Bottom: The great hall stood against the curtain wall to the south of the Great Kitchen Tower, where its foundations can still be traced. The roof was originally supported on ten corbels, of which two survive to indicate the height of the hall and its decoration.

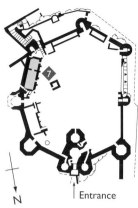

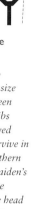

Entrance

N

Originally, there were two vaulted rooms of unequal size in the basement of the Green Chambers. The vaulting ribs were carried on finely carved corbels, three of which survive in damaged form. In the northern room there is a defaced maiden's head (top left), while in the southern room there is the head of an imp (top right) and, in spite of considerable erosion, a splendid lion's mask (right).

Right: This recess in the basement of the Green Chambers is equipped with a drain through the curtain wall and was probably a sink. The presence of this, other drains and benching suggests that the rooms were used for the storage of wine and meat.

Opposite: The Green Chambers probably take their name from the greenish Gwespyr stone that was used in their construction, probably around the mid-fourteenth century. Although little survives of the upper floor, the suite of rooms that it contained must have provided the finest accommodation in the castle.

The turret was called the Pitcher House in 1561, making it probable that pitchers of water, brought from the well in the Goblin Tower, were stored here.

The postern gate provided the most direct means of access to this never-failing supply, particularly necessary in summer when the castle well was exhausted. Halfway up the postern's steps, a stairway led to the upper floor of the Green Chambers. Near the top of the steps, a further short stairway gave access to the first floor of the White Chamber Tower. Within the courtyard, a gallery linked the great hall with the first-floor level of the Green Chambers, supported on the detached north-west buttress.

Green Chambers

The Green Chambers were built against the southern stretch of the east curtain wall, and probably date from the mid-fourteenth century. The name first occurs in 1362–63 and most likely refers to the use of Gwespyr stone, which has a greenish tinge. In the basement there were two vaulted rooms of unequal size, both well lit and both entered separately by steps leading from the courtyard. The presence of drains running out through the curtain (found on excavation), together with benching, suggests the storage of wine and meat. A large recess in the curtain wall at this level still retains a drain and could have housed a sink. The vaulting ribs were carried on carved corbels, which are the finest surviving stonework details in the private apartments. In the north room (in the far corner) is a maiden's head; in the south room are an imp's head and a lion's mask.

The details of the upper floor are less obvious, but the north room contained a fireplace cut into the curtain wall. This suite of rooms provided the finest lodgings in the castle, well worthy of its baronial builders.

Turning left beyond the Green Chambers, visitors will notice that the castle wall joined the town wall at an acute angle. A later wall closed the third side within this area and protected the castle defences at the point where the drains from the Green Chambers emptied into a deep gully. This triangular pit was then vaulted and at an upper level would have provided an additional defensive platform for the town wall. The ruined circular stair, sited at the south-east angle of the Green Chambers, gave access to this platform, and from it one can inspect the gully and drainage system.

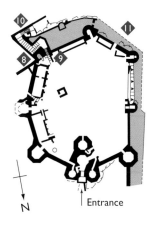

N | Entrance

Below left: The Postern Tower [A] was one of the half-round towers built during the first phase of work at Denbigh. It now marks the junction between the castle and town walls. Adjoining it on the west (right) are the remains of the upper gate [B] .

Below right: The two-storey postern, or lower, gate provided not only a second entrance, but also additional protection for the castle at its weakest point.

Postern Tower 8

This tower stands at the south-east angle of the castle courtyard. It was one of the original towers on the town wall, standing at the point where the town and castle walls now meet. The half-round plan is clear internally; above the basement it stood three storeys high. Externally, it has been considerably strengthened when an elaborate system of outer defences was constructed after the suppression of the 1294–95 revolt. This outer defence consisted of two gates with drawbridges, to which was later added a third gate at the barbican leading from the castle into the outer ditch.

Upper Gate 9

Adjoining the Postern Tower on the west (right) was a gatehouse — the upper gate. Although this gatehouse has almost entirely disappeared, the two pits for the drawbridge and its counterpoise (see reconstruction drawing, p. 33) are visible beneath the modern wooden bridge.

Running southward from the eastern side of the Postern Tower is the wall that formed one side of a steep passage descending to the lower gate; the wall forming the other flank ran from the west side of the upper gate (see reconstruction drawing). The passage has steps for pedestrians on the left side and, originally, it had a sloping ramp for horses on the right. This broad passage could be commanded from both the Postern Tower and the lower gate. Buttressing added to the external face of the Postern Tower improved visibility for the defenders and made the tower far less vulnerable.

Postern Gate 10

The postern, or lower, gate was not only intended to provide a second means of entry to the castle, but also to serve as an extra defence at its weakest point where the rock ridge was most accessible to attackers. The gate was a two-storey tower, but now only the arch springers on the sides of the gate-passage remain to indicate its position. The tower was situated at a point where defenders could control the passage where it makes a right-angled turn (see reconstruction).

Few internal details survive: the wall-passage from the north, the guard-chamber on the north-west, and

An imaginative reconstruction illustrating the relationship between the upper gate and the postern gate, both of which were constructed when the southern defences of the castle were strengthened after Madog's rebellion in 1294–95. Any attacker who attempted to force this entrance would have had to pass through the obstacles in the postern gate — drawbridge, portcullis and double-leaf door. They would also have had to negotiate the three bends of the steep sloping passage while under attack from the Postern Tower and the wall-walk connecting the two gates. At the top of the passage, the upper gate was protected with a drawbridge and a portcullis (Illustration by Chris Jones-Jenkins, 1990).

a latrine shaft hidden behind the outer east wall. The drawbridge and counterpoise pits and the bridge pivot seatings are visible. Beyond these are the much slighter walls of the later barbican.

Mantlet

An outer line of defences was formed by a series of terraces running below the southern and western walls of the castle, between the Postern Tower and the Exchequer Gate. These formed a 'mantle' or cloak to protect the castle where it lacked the additional defence of the town to act as an outer ward, and where the curtain wall of the original period of construction was thinner

and lower than the subsequent work on the north and east.

The mantlet prevented the bases of these half-round towers from being undermined by providing a retaining wall in front of the rock face. Beyond this, there was an outer bank constructed of smaller stones and quarry debris, which made access by siege engines difficult and also hindered the use of battering rams.

Visitors will best appreciate the arrangement in the section of the mantlet between the Postern and Treasure House Towers, which is reached by an opening beside the upper gate. The two towers and their linking curtain wall commanded a clear view of the mantlet. In the retaining wall below, a centrally placed projecting bastion overlooked the approach to the postern gate. At Harlech, a similar bastion may be seen on the outer ward wall.

The mantlet, or low protective screen wall, that was erected to strengthen the castle's southern defences after 1295. A mantlet was also constructed on the western side of the castle (see pp. 2, 8).

A view along the west curtain wall from the Tower-next-Treasure-House towards the Red Tower in the distance.

Treasure House Tower

Back inside the courtyard, and turning left, the visitor comes to the Treasure House Tower. It is of similar design and date to the Postern Tower. The ground-floor room was the Treasure House, in which the records of the lordship of Denbigh were stored. Access to the two upper floors would originally have been from the wall-walks, but a stair was later added to the inner face of the tower to improve access from the courtyard.

In the courtyard along the west and north curtain walls are the foundations of a number of lean-to buildings. They are less substantial than the lodgings and great hall on the east side of the courtyard, and probably represent the stables, smithy and storehouses for the garrison.

Tower-next-Treasure-House

This tower was semicircular on the outside but contained a rectangular room with a large window recess at basement level. It formerly stood three storeys high.

The second stretch of the mantlet was approached through an original opening midway along the curtain wall between the Treasure House Tower and the next tower. The mantlet was divided into sections by cross walls to aid defence and to isolate attackers.

Bishop's Tower ⬥14

Like the Tower-next-Treasure-House, the Bishop's Tower formed part of the original town defences. It was much the same as its neighbour but has been almost entirely destroyed. Its mantlet defence was probably similar, but is here marked by an elaborate defended exit or sally port through which surprise attacks could be launched by defenders, or by which messengers could be sent secretly to obtain fresh supplies and reinforcements.

The sally port (see reconstruction) consists of narrow winding stairs and a passage leading down and out through the base of the mantlet. The passage was defended at the foot of the stair by a portcullis and an inner door with a sharp turn in the passage. Each of the two short lengths of the passage has a murder hole in the roof. No trace survives either of an outer door to the passage or of an upper housing for the portcullis mechanism. Presumably, access to this housing was obtained by a wall-passage leading from the basement of the Bishop's Tower along a bridge onto the mantlet.

Red Tower ⬥15

The Red Tower has an octagonal plan, and owes its name to the liberal use of red sandstone. It was given this name as early as 1374. Steps once led down into the basement room, and to the left more steps led to the two upper floors and to the wall-walks. To the right of the basement entry a passage set in the thickness of the wall provided a defensive route to the Exchequer Gate on the town wall. Although the Red Tower is obviously part of the second phase of the defences and is probably later than the gatehouse, there is no evidence for the half-round tower which presumably preceded it.

A courtyard building stood in the angle between this tower and the gatehouse; holes where corbels have been removed from the curtain wall and a roof seating on the Prison Tower provide evidence for either a courthouse or an armoury.

Above: An artist's impression of the cleverly contrived sally port, which gave access to and from the castle in secret. This discreet exit was protected by a portcullis and murder holes above the passage (Illustration by Chris Jones-Jenkins, 1990).

Left: A view along the stretch of the town wall that connected the Red Tower (the remains of which are visible in the background) with the Exchequer Gate and the rest of the borough defences.

A Tour of Denbigh Town Walls

The greater part of the town walls survives, but visitors are particularly recommended to visit the stretch which includes the Countess Tower and the Goblin Tower. Access to the town walls should be arranged via the custodian at the castle or keys may be borrowed from the library in High Street.

The circuit enclosing the town extends for some 1,200 yards (1,100m), with two twin-towered gates and four towers at irregular intervals. The walls were erected simultaneously with the castle's outer western and southern wall between 1282 and 1294. The gates and the salient — the additional protective wall — at the Goblin Tower date from the fourteenth century, as do the rooms in the Countess Tower.

The eastern section of the town walls (highlighted on the plan) is open — a key can be obtained from the castle or the town library. The town walls have rough stone flooring and no benches. There are numerous flights of steps, some slippery, and very few handrails.

Starting from Cadw's car park go past St Hilary's Chapel down a steep road to the Burgess Gate, which houses an exhibition. Next go along Leicester Terrace to go onto the walls through a locked gate. At the end of the walls there is a steep climb with steps through woodland to emerge back at the car park.

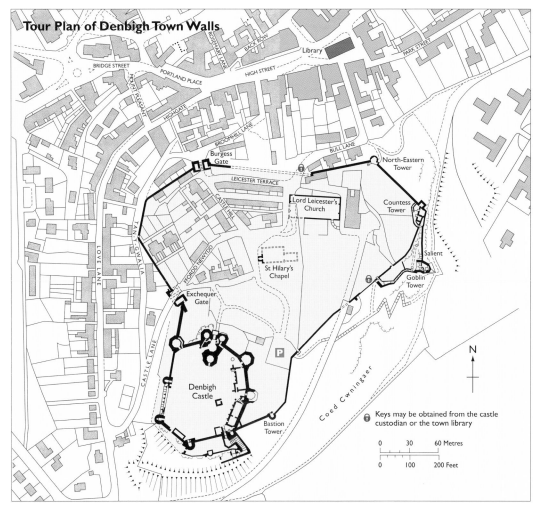

Tour Plan of Denbigh Town Walls

Keys may be obtained from the castle custodian or the town library

Opposite: Denbigh's impressive circuit of town walls was built during the first period of construction, between 1282 and 1294, and the greater part survives to this day. In this view looking towards the Countess Tower, the town wall can be seen running behind the salient, a later protective wall.

Above: The fourteenth-century Burgess Gate was the principal entrance to the town and its importance is emphasized by the chequer-work design of the masonry. The well-protected entrance passage was originally approached by a bridge across a ditch. The first floor was occupied by two interconnecting rooms and there was access from the gate to the wall-walks on either side.

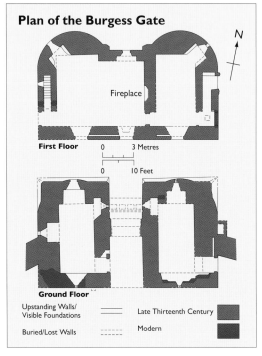

Plan of the Burgess Gate

N

Fireplace

First Floor   0   3 Metres

0   10 Feet

Ground Floor

Upstanding Walls/
Visible Foundations   Late Thirteenth Century

Buried/Lost Walls   Modern

Exchequer Gate

The stretch of wall linking the Red Tower to the Exchequer Gate does not stand to any great height. The gate is represented only by its excavated foundations visible through railings either side of the modern road. These show a twin-towered gate of rectangular plan at the base, probably round-fronted at first-floor level and looking very similar to the Burgess Gate. The street level of Ffordd Newydd now runs through the gate at its first-floor level. The gate was close enough to the castle to receive additional protection from the Red Tower and the great gatehouse.

The north-west stretch between the Exchequer Gate and the Burgess Gate stands complete but is hidden behind the houses in Tan-y-Gwalia. There is no evidence for towers at the points where the wall changes direction.

Burgess Gate

The Burgess Gate stands at the west end of the long northern stretch of the town wall and was originally approached by a bridge crossing a ditch. The entrance is flanked by projecting towers, the eastern one of which may have contained a vaulted guard chamber, while the western one had a timber ceiling. The vaulted entrance passage had doors at the centre with a portcullis in front. The doorway itself was further protected by four murder holes in the vault above and arrowloops on either side of the passageway. On the first floor, the gatehouse was divided into two intercommunicating rooms. The smaller chamber to the east occupied the width of the eastern tower only and was equipped with a latrine; the larger room to the west, with a fireplace, extended over the gatehouse passage. From the western tower, a stair in the thickness of the wall led from the first floor to the roof. There was also access from the gate to the wall-walk on either side.

The variety of the building stone distinguishes this gate from the main curtain wall. The stones used are the greyish white Carboniferous limestone and the greenish yellow sandstone from Pont Lawnt, a mile (1.6km) south-west of the town. The chequer-work design of the stones emphasizes the importance of this gateway, the principal entrance to the town and the symbol of urban pride.

Denbigh Castle from the north-east, published by Samuel and Nathaniel Buck in 1742. The salient and the Goblin Tower, which were added to the borough fortifications in the fourteenth century, occupy the foreground.

The town wall between the Burgess Gate and the new church built by Lord Leicester has nearly all been destroyed, but the next section is well preserved and open to visitors. A key available from the castle custodian or the library is required to enter the northern stretch (please remember to lock the gate). It runs eastward to the north-eastern tower, a half-round structure now of two storeys with a latrine chute on the east. The wall then turns through 120 degrees, descending south-easterly to reach the Countess Tower.

Countess Tower

This tower probably takes its name from a fourteenth-century countess of March. It consists of two angular turrets to which have been added two rooms within the angle of the wall. The north turret is a square room of two storeys with a fireplace in the south-east angle and above it a dovecote — which may be later. The east turret was a larger room of two storeys. There are the remains of a fireplace in the south wall of the lower storey. Another room was later added south of the east turret, within the original town wall, and beyond this, a doorway with a portcullis groove gave access to the salient protecting the well in the Goblin Tower.

This salient enclosed a triangular piece of ground along the face of the rock, placed forward from the original town wall. On the east side of the salient, the curtain wall linking the Countess and Goblin Towers had a double series of embrasures with the upper line reached by a narrow wall-walk and the lower line approached from the pathway between the two towers.

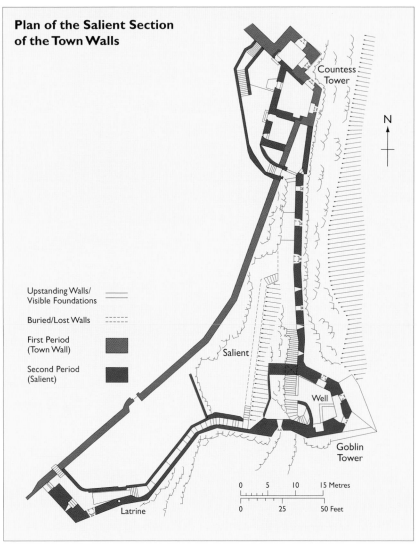

Plan of the Salient Section of the Town Walls

Countess Tower

N

Upstanding Walls/
Visible Foundations

Buried/Lost Walls

First Period
(Town Wall)

Second Period
(Salient)

Salient

Well

Goblin
Tower

| 0 | 5 | 10 | 15 Metres |

| 0 | 25 | 50 Feet |

Latrine

Goblin Tower

The Goblin Tower is a large, irregular, hexagonal bastion projecting from the face of the limestone cliff. It is of two main storeys with a narrow stairway descending from the lower floor to a deep well. The lower floor has the main entrance on the north approached by a flight of steps continuing the pathway leading down from the Countess Tower. The upper storey was reached by a staircase on the south wall. The tower has a fireplace set in the angle between the south wall and the face of the cliff served by an ingeniously placed smoke escape shaft.

The well mechanism was probably housed at the level of the lower floor, but might have been in a well house on the tower roof to eliminate too much labour in carrying water buckets to the castle itself. Looking northwards along the outer face of this tower, you can see the glacis — the sloping masonry bank that protects the base of the curtain wall from attack.

The present footpath climbs up from the Goblin Tower and runs in line with the southern wall of the salient. This wall was originally reached by a circular stair from the Goblin Tower and a wall-walk must have run at a somewhat higher level than today's pathway. The wall-walk continued upwards to enter a postern gate protecting the junction between the original town wall and the new salient defences. The wall-walk was entered by a drawbridge at the level of the floor within the new postern turret. The drawbridge pit is still visible, and the defences involved two sharp turns within the turret.

Bastion Tower

As visitors continue to climb the path through the wood and up towards the castle, they will notice that beyond the end of the salient there are no further defensive towers until the Bastion Tower is reached. This infrequency of interval towers at baronial boroughs, as at Cowbridge, Vale of Glamorgan, and at Tenby, Pembrokeshire, is in marked contrast to their frequency at the royal boroughs of Conwy and Caernarfon.

The path leads up towards a stone stile on the line of the walls via steep stone steps and, by turning left, the visitor arrives at the car park beyond which lies the Bastion Tower (not accessible). It is a half-round structure, similar to the Postern Tower to its west; it has a basement and probably had three upper storeys. Like the Burgess Gate it is attractively decorated externally with a chequer-work pattern of fawn sandstone alternating with white limestone. Please remember to return the key for the gates on the town walls before you leave.

An artist's reconstruction of the salient and Goblin Tower in the fourteenth century. The lower floor of the Goblin Tower gave access to a deep well — which provided a dependable source of water throughout the year (Illustration by Chris Jones-Jenkins, 1990).

Opposite: The salient and Goblin Tower today, from a similar viewpoint.

Lord Leicester's Church

A steep tarmac road leads from the castle down to Lord Leicester's Church. The interior is not currently accessible.

Robert Dudley, earl of Leicester and Baron Denbigh (1564–88), decided to build a new church more fitting to his dignity as virtual governor of north Wales. It is traditionally held that Dudley intended his new church to replace St Asaph as the cathedral in north-east Wales. King Edward I had had a similar idea of replacing St Asaph with a new cathedral at Rhuddlan in 1284. Bishop Henry Standish of St Asaph (1518–35), too, had proposed to move the cathedral to Wrexham in the 1530s.

Building work on the church proceeded slowly despite appeals to all English bishops to collect funds throughout their dioceses in 1579–80. According to the historian, Thomas Pennant, writing in 1786–89, 'Leicester left off his buildings in Wales, by reason of the public hatred he had incurred on account of his tyranny. A sum was afterwards collected in order to complete the work; but it is said that when the earl of Essex passed through Denbigh on his Irish expedition he borrowed money destined for the purpose, which was never repaid; and by that means the church was left unfinished.'

The new church was a large rectangular structure, 170 feet by 72 feet (52m by 22m) internally, with a broad central aisle 27 feet (8.2m) wide and narrower side aisles. The church was almost certainly divided into a chancel of three bays and a nave of seven bays with circular piers set on square plinths. No details of the internal ritual arrangements remain.

The north wall stands up to roof height with nine plain window openings. The westernmost bay has a four-centred doorway with red sandstone mouldings. A foundation stone of 1578 and a dedication stone of 1579 survived for at least 200 years.

Above: The title page of the first complete Welsh translation of the Bible, which was published by William Morgan (d. 1604) in 1588. Although he held the post as a sinecure, Morgan was the first vicar of Lord Leicester's Church from 1575 to 1596 (National Library of Wales).

Right: Lord Leicester's Church was the only large new church to be built in Britain during the Elizabethan period.

Robert Dudley, Earl of Leicester

There is no firm evidence that Lord Leicester spent much on the castle at Denbigh, unlike his main residence at Kenilworth, near Warwick, and his London house at Wanstead in Essex. It was at these two establishments that the flamboyant earl organized pageants, masques and water entertainments with the help of the poet, Edmund Spenser (d. 1599).

It was to these houses, too, that Protestant poets, painters and preachers came, and where Puritan refugees from France and the Netherlands were sheltered. It was from there that Lord Leicester set out to win military glory as the protector of the Dutch Protestants, who were fighting against the Catholic Spanish in the Netherlands. It was to Lord Leicester's Hospital in Warwick that the wounded soldiers came to find generous lodging in newly built accommodation.

Leicester, the queen's favourite, shared her Protestant beliefs but he was more strongly supportive of the Presbyterians and the Puritans who favoured spontaneous preaching or 'prophesying'. Between 1570 and 1577 he encouraged such activities with the appointment of his private chaplains and the promotion of bishops who shared his views. The preaching church at Denbigh was founded in 1578 to foster 'teachers sufficientlie to convince the gainesaier'. From 1577 to 1584 Leicester took a less prominent role at court, but he was still regarded as 'the cherisher and patron-general' of the Puritans.

His death, aged 56, in 1588 was mourned by all Puritans, but may have been welcomed by the Welsh as the passing of another English oppressor.

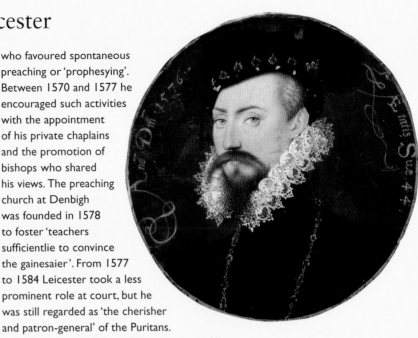

A 1576 miniature of the earl of Leicester by Nicholas Hilliard (d. 1619) (National Portrait Gallery, London).

Externally, the building is plain and reflects the character of the more Puritan Protestant worship conducted within. The only decorations were the simple sandstone quoins at the four corners of the church and the simple roll moulding below the base of the window openings. These windows when filled with clear glass would have given a purified appearance, enabling the worshippers to follow the services in their prayer books. The first vicar here (as a sinecure 1575–96) was William Morgan (d. 1604), who translated the whole Bible into Welsh for the first time and published it in 1588.

The interest of this church lies in the fact that it is the only large new church in Britain of the Elizabethan period and is the first Protestant building, intended for a preaching ministry, to be erected on a new site. It precedes St Katharine Cree in London and Londonderry Cathedral by thirty years. These are all of traditional rectangular hall-church plan, unlike the innovations of the Dutch Reformers who built circular or octagonal structures.

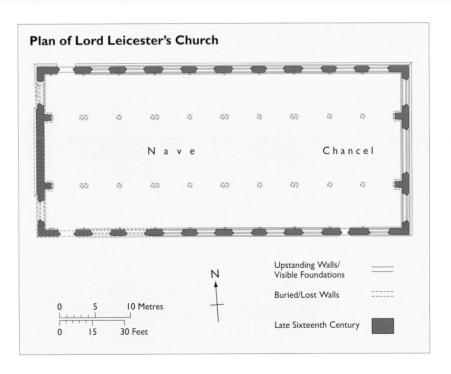

Plan of Lord Leicester's Church

Nave   Chancel

N

| 0 | 5 | 10 Metres |
| 0 | 15 | 30 Feet |

Upstanding Walls/ Visible Foundations ——————

Buried/Lost Walls - - - - - -

Late Sixteenth Century ▪

St Hilary's Chapel

The chapel serving the town was erected in a central position within the town walls, midway between the Burgess Gate and the castle gatehouse. It was ecclesiastically dependent on Whitchurch (Llanfarchell), the mother church of this area, situated on the valley floor. It was referred to in 1334 as 'the chapel within the walls'.

In the new towns of the Edwardian conquest the provision of churches for English immigrant town dwellers was a necessity, but posed problems of space and of legal status. In Caernarfon and Flint the chapels were small in size, tucked in odd corners of the town and dependent on an older mother church. At Ruthin and Rhuddlan, new churches were built,

The west tower is all that remains of St Hilary's Chapel — the 'chapel within the walls' mentioned in a document of 1334. It was erected to serve the needs of the English immigrants who settled in Henry de Lacy's borough. It did not finally fall into disuse until 1874, though Lord Leicester had intended to replace it with his great new preaching hall, the ruins of which are visible in the background.

while at Conwy the existing Cistercian abbey church was converted to parochial use after the monks had been transferred to a new site.

Only the tower of St Hilary's now remains, but the position of the chapel is marked by the level terrace east of the tower; the fall of the ground enabled a crypt to be built beneath the eastern half. It was a large building with a nave of five bays, a north aisle and a shorter, narrower chancel. The chapel was originally built about 1300, soon after the town's foundation, but many of the window openings were enlarged in the Perpendicular style and the north aisle was entirely rebuilt in 1707–11, using stone from Lord Leicester's Church.

The unbuttressed tower is of three stages, 16 feet (4.9m) square and 46 feet (14.1m) high. There is a west doorway of about 1300, and single lights at the second stage on both north and south faces, and double lights at the belfry stage on all four faces; the uppermost 5 feet (1.5m) of masonry with the battlemented top is fifteenth century in date. The west gable of the nave remains with a blocked four-centred arch separating the tower from the nave.

It was this town chapel that Lord Leicester intended to replace with his great new preaching hall, more in keeping with the Protestant form of worship. However, St Hilary's only finally fell into disuse when a new town church was built in 1874. It was demolished in 1923 leaving the tower standing alone.

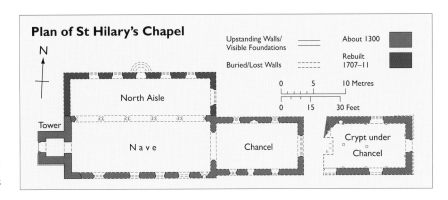

Plan of St Hilary's Chapel

Upstanding Walls/Visible Foundations — About 1300

Buried/Lost Walls --- Rebuilt 1707–11

0   5   10 Metres
0   15   30 Feet

Tower | North Aisle | Nave | Chancel | Crypt under Chancel

SECTION A-A

Above: Before the nave and chancel of St Hilary's were demolished in 1923, the building was carefully surveyed. This section across the nave and north aisle provides useful information on decorative details and internal structure.

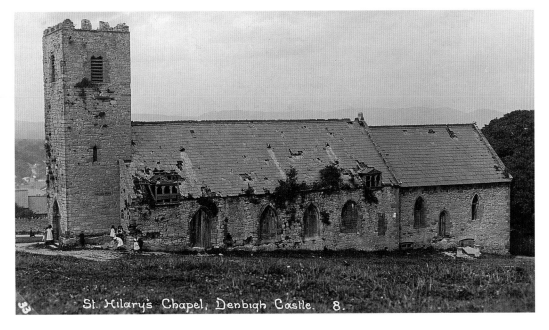

St. Hilary's Chapel, Denbigh Castle.   8.

Left: A photograph of St Hilary's prior to its demolition.

Denbigh Friary

Friars were religious men, but, unlike monks, did not live their lives within the cloister; nor did they support themselves by the ownership of property. They were itinerant and they were mendicant; that is, they moved from place to place and were expected to beg for their livelihood. They were to live in poverty, in imitation of the Apostles, teaching and preaching by word and example. The Carmelites, or white friars, were originally founded as a hermit group on Mount Carmel in Palestine, around 1210. They arrived in England in the mid-thirteenth century, apparently as a consequence of invitations by lay patrons, and as their reliance on begging and scholarly pursuits increased, they gravitated towards towns where most new houses were established.

The house of the white friars in Denbigh was founded late in the thirteenth century and may have been established in 1289 under the patronage of John de Swynmore. Here, their simple life of poverty would have been an inspiration to other poor Christians and a rebuke to the ostentatious rich. Their scholarship and learned preaching would have supplemented the few sermons of the local parish priests and so their message would have spread around the lordship of Denbigh.

In the later Middle Ages the friary enjoyed the especial patronage of the Salusbury family of Lleweni and Bachymbyd, many of whom were buried here.

It also had the support of the bishops of St Asaph. Bishop Henry Standish (1518–35), was a Carmelite friar: he gave generously to this house and lived here in 'the bishops chamber'. He was followed by Robert Purefoy who also preferred to live here. At the surrender of the house in 1538, on the orders of Henry VIII (1509–47), four friars were in residence. The friary buildings included a 'quyer' (choir), vestry, chamber, hall, kitchen, brewhouse and buttery.

The surviving building is the greater part of the church. The friars' choir stands up to roof height.

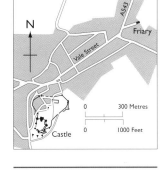

Denbigh Friary is located about 2 miles (7km) from the castle, just off the A543. A rough, level track provides access to the paved nave and chancel.

Opposite: The interior of the church of the Carmelite friary that was founded on the north-eastern outskirts of Denbigh in the thirteenth century. The large east window, now filled with brick to support the tracery, would have illuminated the friars' choir.

Above left: Carmelite, or white, friars at their devotions, from a fifteenth-century book of hours (Bibliothèque Nationale de France, Paris, Ms. Latin 1176, f. 132).

Left: This 1742 engraving of the friary church by Samuel and Nathaniel Buck shows that it was still roofed, with the base of its wooden steeple or belfry visible.

The large east window (now with a modern brick infill to give support) was altered early in the fifteenth century to give more light. Another large window (also with a brick infill) in the north wall is set high up to avoid the stalls of the brothers, as is the case on the south wall. The stone seats and sink (sedilia and piscina) in the south-east corner are part of the original construction.

West of the large windows a timber screen would have divided the choir from a lobby or 'walking place' with a wooden steeple or belfry above it. This belfry is shown on Speed's map of 1610 (p. 17: K — The Abbey). Beyond the walking place and the south door, which led into the cloister, was the nave for the lay folk. Two altars stood against a second screen and in the south wall is the piscina which served the southern altar. A well was dug after the friary had closed and its houses had been turned into farm buildings.

Three ranges of domestic buildings provided the living quarters for the friars around the cloister to the south. This was 'halfe-overbuylded', as was normal in friaries, meaning that the upper floors extended over the cloister walk, unlike the abbeys of monks where the cloister walks were lean-to corridors set against the ranges of the cloister. On the east side was the chapter house and the bishop's chamber; on the south side stood the dormitory, probably with the refectory on the ground floor; on the west side was the hall, either the refectory or a guest hall. The kitchen and brewhouse would be close to the refectory and the guest house; there would be barns and stabling in an outer court. Abbey Cottage occupies the position of the south range and incorporates some of its fabric.

The best example of a friary church in Wales is at Brecon, where the Dominican, or black friars, church is in use as the school chapel at Christ College.

Plan of Denbigh Friary

N

Well

Nave   Screen   Steeple (over)   Screen   Choir

0   3   6 Metres

0   10   20 Feet

Site of Cloister

Upstanding Walls/ Visible Foundations ——

Buried/Lost Walls ------

Late Thirteenth Century

Fourteenth Century

Late Fifteenth Century

Modern

Site of Altar +

Right: The sedilia in the south wall of the choir provided seating for the clergy celebrating the Mass. The piscina, to the left, was a sink used by the priest to cleanse the chalice and paten (plate) after Mass.

The finest example of a friary church in Wales is the school chapel at Christ College, Brecon. It was built in the thirteenth century for a community of Dominican friars (Christ College, Brecon).

Further Reading

Acknowledgements

The author and Cadw would like to thank Richard Brewer, Dr John Goodall and Professor Ralph Griffiths for their assistance with the text.

L. A. S. Butler, 'Lord Leicester's Church, Denbigh: An Experiment in Puritan Worship', *Journal of the British Archaeological Association*, 3rd Series, **37** (1974), 40–62.

A. W. Clapham, 'The Architectural Remains of the Mendicant Orders in Wales', *The Archaeological Journal* **36** (1927), 101–04.

R. R. Davies, *Conquest, Coexistence, and Change: Wales 1063–1415* (Oxford 1987); reprinted in paperback as *The Age of Conquest: Wales 1063–1415* (Oxford 1991).

R. R. Davies, *The Revolt of Owain Glyn Dŵr* (Oxford 1995).

W. J. Hemp, 'Denbigh Castle', *Y Cymmrodor* **36** (1926), 64–120.

E. Neaverson, *Mediaeval Castles in North Wales* (Liverpool 1947).

D. H. Owen, 'Denbigh', in R. A. Griffiths, editor, *Boroughs of Mediaeval Wales* (Cardiff 1978), 165–87.

C. Smith, 'The Excavation of the Exchequer Gate, Denbigh, 1982–83', *Archaeologia Cambrensis* **137** (1988), 108–12.

A. Taylor, *The Welsh Castles of Edward I* (London 1986).

N. Tucker, 'Denbigh's Loyal Governor', *Transactions of the Denbighshire Historical Society* **5** (1956), 7–34.

G. Williams, *Recovery, Reorientation and Reformation: Wales c. 1415–1642* (Oxford 1987); reprinted in paperback as *Renewal and Reformation: Wales c. 1415–1642* (Oxford 1993).